A FIRST LOOK AT CATERPILLARS

A FIRST LOOK AT CATERPILLARS

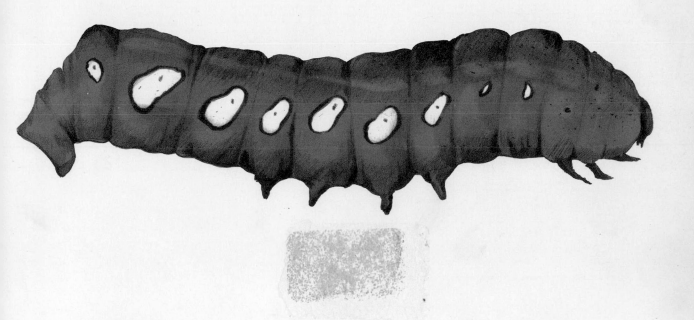

By Millicent E. Selsam and Joyce Hunt

Illustrated by Harriett Springer

WALKER AND COMPANY ✳ NEW YORK

First published in the United States of America in 1987 by the Walker
Publishing Company, Inc.

Published simultaneously in Canada by Thomas Allen & Son
Canada, Limited, Markham, Ontario

Library of Congress Cataloging-in-Publication Data

Selsam, Millicent Ellis, 1912–
    A first look at caterpillars.

    (A First look at series)
    Summary: Briefly describes the live cycle and habitat of the
caterpillar.
    1. Caterpillars—Juvenile literature.
[1. Caterpillars] I. Hunt, Joyce. II. Springer, Harriett,
ill. III. Title. IV. Series: Selsam, Millicent Ellis, 1912–
        First look at series.
QL544.2.S45 1987   595.78'0439   87-18999
ISBN 0-8027-6700-1
ISBN 0-8027-6702-8 (lib. bdg.)

Printed in the United States of America

10 9 8 7 6 5 4 3 2 1

A *FIRST LOOK AT* SERIES

A FIRST LOOK AT LEAVES
A FIRST LOOK AT FISH
A FIRST LOOK AT MAMMALS
A FIRST LOOK AT BIRDS
A FIRST LOOK AT INSECTS
A FIRST LOOK AT FROGS AND TOADS
A FIRST LOOK AT SNAKES, LIZARDS, AND OTHER REPTILES
A FIRST LOOK AT ANIMALS WITH BACKBONES
A FIRST LOOK AT ANIMALS WITHOUT BACKBONES
A FIRST LOOK AT FLOWERS
A FIRST LOOK AT THE WORLD OF PLANTS
A FIRST LOOK AT MONKEYS AND APES
A FIRST LOOK AT SHARKS
A FIRST LOOK AT WHALES
A FIRST LOOK AT CATS
A FIRST LOOK AT DOGS
A FIRST LOOK AT HORSES
A FIRST LOOK AT SEASHELLS
A FIRST LOOK AT DINOSAURS
A FIRST LOOK AT SPIDERS
A FIRST LOOK AT ROCKS
A FIRST LOOK AT BIRD NESTS
A FIRST LOOK AT KANGAROOS, KOALAS,
    AND OTHER ANIMALS WITH POUCHES
A FIRST LOOK AT OWLS, EAGLES, AND OTHER
    HUNTERS OF THE SKY
A FIRST LOOK AT POISONOUS SNAKES
A FIRST LOOK AT CATERPILLARS

Each of the nature books in this series is planned to develop the child's powers of observation—to train him or her to notice distinguishing characteristics. A leaf is a leaf. A bird is a bird. An insect is an insect. That is true. But what makes an oak leaf different from a maple leaf? Why is a hawk different from an eagle, or a beetle different from a bug?

Classification is a painstaking science. These books give a child the essence of the search for differences that is the basis for scientific classification.

For Ethan

The authors wish to thank Mr. Louis Sorkin of the
Department of Entomology of the American Museum
of Natural History for reading the text of this book
and for offering many helpful suggestions.

Butterflies and moths laid these eggs.

Some look like tiny ears of corn.
Some look like green peas.
Some look like grapes.

From the different eggs come different caterpillars.

This is what a caterpillar looks like close up.

The Parts of a Caterpillar

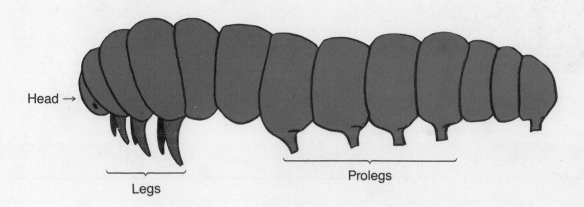

Head →

Legs

Prolegs

Most caterpillars have 3 pairs of legs.
They also have other parts that look like legs.
These are called prolegs.

Their bodies are usually divided into 12 segments (parts).
Count them.

Is this a caterpillar?

No, it is a worm.
Worms have no legs.
Besides, a worm is a worm all its life,
but caterpillars change.

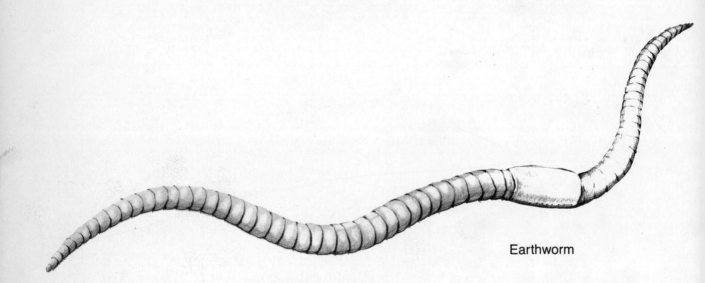

Earthworm

Some caterpillars change into butterflies.

Some caterpillars change into moths.

All caterpillars do not look the same.
How do you tell them apart?

Some are long and thin.
Some are short and fat.
Some are smooth, some have bumps,
some are hairy.

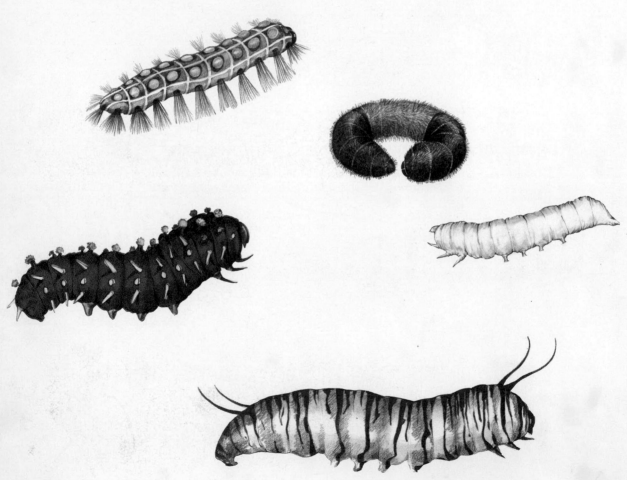

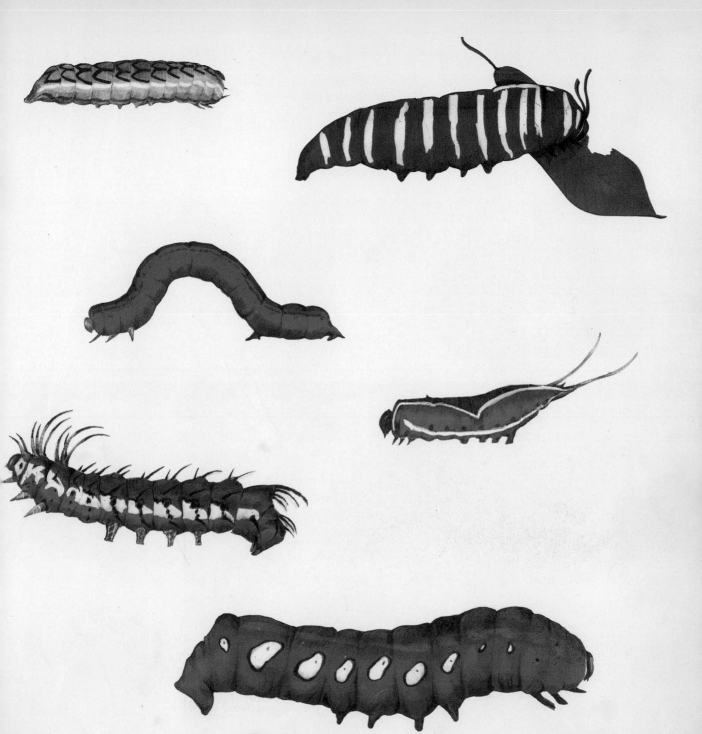

13

CATERPILLARS THAT BECOME MOTHS

Many moth caterpillars are hairy.
Find the caterpillar with tufts of hair that look
like brushes.
Find the caterpillar with hair all over its body.

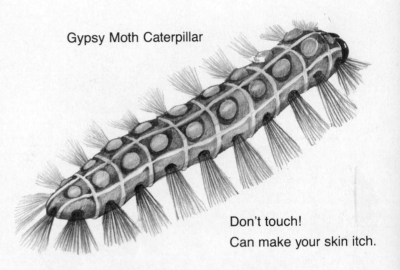

Gypsy Moth Caterpillar

Wooly Bear
Rolls into a ball when disturbed.

Don't touch!
Can make your skin itch.

This one is so hairy that you can't even see
its head.

Puss Moth Caterpillar

Don't touch this one, either.
It also makes you itch.

Other moth caterpillars are spiny.
The *Cecropia* (suh-*kro*-pee-a) caterpillar
has both spines and bumps.
The *Hickory Horned Devil*
has both spines and "horns."
Which is which?

You can tell some caterpillars by their names:

Match the caterpillar to its name:

WHITE CUTWORM

STRIPED CUTWORM

W-MARKED CUTWORM

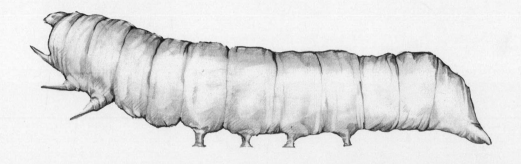

17

You can tell one caterpillar from another by the way it holds its body.

Which one holds its middle section up
as it loops along a stem?

Which one holds its front end up?

Which one holds its rear end up?

Prominent Moth Caterpillar

Tomato Hornworm

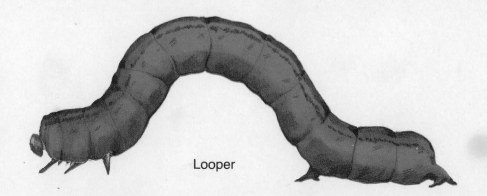

Looper

19

The *Silk Caterpillar* lives in Asia.
The cocoon it forms is made of a single thread
of silk that can be almost a mile long.
The silk is used to make clothes.

Other caterpillars eat clothes.
The *Clothes Moth* lays its eggs in wool, fur, or feathers.
When the eggs hatch the young caterpillars eat holes in the clothing.

Some caterpillars live in silky tents.
They rest in the tents and come out to feed.
The Eastern Tent Caterpillar feeds on apple and cherry trees.

Have you ever opened an ear of corn and found
a little caterpillar?
It is called a *Corn Earworm*.

Corn Earworms can destroy whole crops of corn.

Mexican Jumping Beans jump.
The beans are seeds.
Inside the seeds are little caterpillars.
They stay in the seeds all winter.
When they feel warmth they start to move.

CATERPILLARS THAT BECOME BUTTERFLIES

When you see a caterpillar you can not tell whether
it is going to change into a moth or a butterfly.

Butterfly caterpillars can also be long and thin,
short and fat, hairy, striped, or spiny.

This butterfly caterpillar has spines.

Brush-footed Butterfly Caterpillar

Both ends of this striped caterpillar have "horns."

Monarch Butterfly Caterpillar

Swallowtail Caterpillars have horns also.
But they only have them at one end.
Look behind their heads.

Find the black and green Swallowtail Caterpillar
with light spots.

Find the one with light stripes.

Find the green one with a large eyespot.
(Many Swallowtail Caterpillars have eyespots.)

Zebra Swallowtail Caterpillars eat
the leaves of the pawpaw tree.

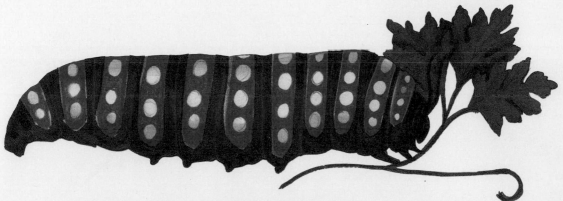

Black Swallowtail Caterpillars eat parsley.

Spicebush Swallowtail Caterpillars eat
the leaves of the sassafras tree.

27

There are other clues to look for that help
tell butterfly caterpillars apart.

Look for the caterpillar with a forked tail.

Look for the one with a thin neck and a large head.

Look for the one with a long stripe.

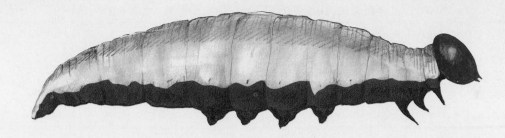

True Skipper

Brown Butterfly Caterpillar

White Butterfly Caterpillar

29

You can raise your own caterpillars.
Look for them on plants.
Big holes in the leaves are signs that
caterpillars are near.
Put one in a jar.
Make holes in the top so that it can breathe.
Feed the caterpillar with the same kind of leaves
it was eating when you found it.
Put a few drops of water on the leaves.

After a few days the caterpillar will stop eating.
If it is a moth caterpillar it will spin a cocoon.
If it is a butterfly caterpillar it will start to
harden and change into a chrysalis (*kriss*-a-liss).
After some time a moth or a butterfly will hatch.
See what happens.

Cocoon   Chrysalis

TO TELL CATERPILLARS APART:

Look for hair.

Look for spines.

Look at the pattern.

Look at the way it holds its body.

Look for "horns."

Look for forked tails.

Look for silky tents.

CATERPILLARS IN THIS BOOK

Black Swallowtail Caterpillar   26–27
Brown Butterfly Caterpillar   28–29
Brush-footed Butterfly Caterpillar   25
Cecropia Moth Caterpillar   15
Clothes Moth Caterpillar   21
Corn Earworm   23
Eastern Tent Caterpillar   22
Gypsy Moth Caterpillar   14
Hickory Horned Devil   15
Looper   18–19
Mexican Jumping Bean   23
Monarch Butterfly Caterpillar   25
Prominent Moth Caterpillar   18–19
Puss Moth Caterpillar   14
Silk Caterpillar   20
Spicebush Swallowtail Caterpillar   26–27
Striped Cutworm   16–17
Tomato Hornworm   18–19
True Skipper Butterfly Caterpillar   28–29
W-Marked Cutworm   16–17
White Butterfly Caterpillar   28–29
White Cutworm   16–17
Wooly Bear   14
Zebra Swallowtail Caterpillar   26–27